CONTENTS

Hello, friends! My name is Hector, and I'd like to invite you to visit a magical place covered in misty mountains, golden wheat fields and olive groves of outstanding beauty. It is a place where the shores are bathed by a glorious blue sea, where the lines are blurred between fantasy and reality, myth and history.

I'm talking about Greece, a land filled with ruins that tell fabulous stories of heroes and goddesses, athletes and thinkers, explorers and poets.

If you put on these glasses, we'll go back in time together and witness the most extraordinary moments in Greek history, which have made a lasting impact on the sciences and the arts, our thoughts and ideas, how we build our cities and even how we live as a society today!

Are you ready? Let's get started ...

Welcome to ancient Greece!

THE ODYSSEAN SEA

The Mediterranean is a sea full of history and tales. One of its most famous stories is **The Odyssey**, which was told by a poet known as **Homer**. It's all about a man called **Odysseus** (or Ulysses to the Romans) and his journey home after battling in the Trojan War (which you can follow on the map below). The story includes some incredible descriptions of the landscape and villages surrounding the ancient Mediterranean.

Ancient Greeks never called themselves 'Greek', this was a Roman word. Instead, they called themselves 'Hellenes', and their land, 'Hellas'.

10
Cimmerians

16 Scheria

9 Aeaea

SARDINIA

15 Ogygia

11 Sirens

MEDITERRANEAN SEA

SPAIN

Aeolis
7

8
Telepylos

Lotus-Eaters

5

The Greeks expanded their territory by colonising many parts of the Mediterranean. From their starting point in **Greece**, their territory stretched all the way to modern-day **Spain** on one side, and then to the west coast of **Asia** and the **Black Sea** on the other. Under the rule of **Alexander the Great**, their empire spread eastwards into Egypt, the Middle East and parts of India.

The ports and trade routes that the Greeks set up turned the Mediterranean into a place where more goods and more people moved around than ever before. Like today, the sea was not always safe, but for those who braved these waters, a fortune could be made. People traded wine from Greece, spices from Byzantium, wheat from Sicily, silver from Tartessos, gold from Africa and cloth from Persia and Phoenicia.

Ideas also moved. As the Greeks expanded their empire, their culture travelled with them. Many people were influenced by the Greek language, ways of life and customs. At the same time, the Greeks also were influenced by the traditions from these communities, which shaped their own identity. By sharing each other's cultures, the region became more connected – like an early version of the diverse, global community we live in today!

ADRIATIC SEA

BLACK SEA

ITALY

GREECE

Ismaros

2

1 Troy

AEGEAN SEA

Scylla

12

13 Charybdis

Ithaca **17**

Islands of the Aegean Sea

6 Cyclops

Cape Matapan

3

4 Kythera

14 Island of Thrinacia

Odysseus

Crete

MEDITERRANEAN SEA

THE STUFF OF LEGENDS

When we call a singer or a footballer a 'legend', we mean they are one-in-a-million and will most certainly go down in history. Greek myths and legends were similar: they told incredible tales about extraordinary beings in times gone by. These stories and adventures were passed on by word of mouth from generation to generation, and later on through art and literature, until they became part of our shared storytelling culture.

But unlike stories about our modern-day celebrities, the classic myths of the ancient Greeks tried to explain the mysteries they saw in world around them, like: How did the world begin? What is the meaning of life? Is there life after death?

Just like other ancient cultures, the Greeks turned to stories to try to find the answers to these questions, creating fascinating tales that made a complex world easier to understand.

Zeus

Hera

Athena

Aphrodite

Apollo

Artemis

Hephaestus

Dionysus

Greek mythology is rich and creative. The ancient Greeks invented a whole host of incredible characters – heroes and goddesses, nymphs and monsters, titans, sirens and centaurs – and wove them into their tales, creating a universe full of action and adventure.

The most well-known of all of these characters were the Olympian gods, so called because they lived on **Mount Olympus**. On top of this mountain, beyond the clouds, was the home of **Zeus** – the master of earth and sky – who reigned alongside his wife **Hera**, the goddess of marriage and family. There were other extraordinary gods and goddesses who lived with them, like **Athena** (goddess of wisdom), **Aphrodite** (goddess of love), **Apollo** (god of the arts and beauty), **Artemis** (goddess of hunting), **Ares** (god of war), **Hephaestus** (god of fire and craftsmanship), **Hermes** (god of trade and travel), **Dionysus** (god of wine and fertility) and **Heracles**, a hero who was transformed into a god when he died.

Zeus had many siblings, like Poseidon (god of the sea), Hades (god of death) and Demeter (goddess of harvest).

7

ARIADNE'S THREAD

Bulls were sacred animals for the Minoans and played a role in their rituals.

START

Island of Crete

Enter the labyrinth and help Theseus find his way to the Minotaur. Use Ariadne's thread to guide you!

Sometimes, it can be difficult to draw a clear line between fact and fiction, or myth and history. If you want an example, just look at the island of Crete. During the **Bronze Age** (which started nearly 2,000 years before the period we know as 'ancient Greece' came to be), this was home to the **Minoans**, a prosperous and thriving culture named after their legendary king, **Minos**.

Tragically, nearly all of the Minoan palaces and monuments were destroyed by a series of natural disasters, combined with an invasion by the **Mycenaeans**, the other most developed and powerful culture of that time.

Recent studies suggest that the Minoans and Mycenaeans are the most direct ancestors of modern-day Greeks.

However, the legacy of the Minoans did not disappear altogether. Their memory and influence are kept alive in Greek culture thanks to myths such as that of the **Minotaur**.

This story tells of a monster – half-human, half-bull – that lived in a **labyrinth** (maze) and ate (gulp!) human flesh. **Theseus**, the great hero of Athens, used a ball of thread belonging to **Princess Ariadne** to guide himself through the labyrinth, slay the beast and find his way back again, safe and sound.

At the beginning of the 20th century, the **Knossos Palace** was unearthed. Knossos was Crete's capital city during the Minoan era. The palace was so complex, with so many rooms and passageways decorated with paintings of bulls, that many people thought they'd actually found the mythical labyrinth of the Minotaur. However, most archaeologists nowadays argue that it was unlikely to be the same place. The Greek philosopher Plato has suggested that the myth of Theseus and the Minotaur may be a metaphor for when we find ourselves in a tricky situation and need all our brainpower to overcome it. If that's the case, perhaps you too have felt like Theseus or Ariadne at some point!

HOW WE KNOW OUR ABCs

Many of the myths told by the ancient Greeks were actually older than ancient Greece itself. For centuries, they were passed down from one generation to the next by word of mouth. We know of these stories today because of the written texts that were created by the Greeks, and later preserved by the Romans and Muslim scholars, so the tales could be retold again and again. The key to all this was the invention of the **Greek alphabet**, which allowed the myths to be written down.

Waxed **tablets** or books

An alphabet is a collection of symbols we use to communicate. It's the basis for a system of writing where each letter represents a certain sound.

Though people have long given credit to the Greeks for inventing their alphabet, like many of their other great inventions, they actually had taken inspiration from another culture. In this case, it was their trading friends the **Phoenicians**. This civilisation lived along the eastern coast of the Mediterranean and already had their own alphabet (though it only used consonants). In the 9th century BCE, the Greeks adapted this alphabet and added in new letters for vowels, which hadn't existed before then. Can you imagine what English would look like without vowels? *Prbbly hrdr t ndrstnd!*

Stylus to write with

α	β	γ	δ
A alpha	B beta	G gamma	D delta
ε	ζ	η	θ
E epsilon	Z zeta	E eta	C/Z theta
ι	κ	λ	μ
I iota	C/K kappa	L lambda	M mu
ν	ξ	o	π
N nu	X xi	omicron	P pi
ρ	σ	τ	υ
R rho	S sigma	T tau	U upsilon
φ	χ	ψ	ω
F phi	J chi	S psi	O omega

The ancient Greeks wrote a lot, and for lots of reasons – to keep records, to express ideas, to create great works of art – but that didn't mean everyone could read and write. In fact, historians think that only 20–30 per cent of all Greeks were literate. Luckily, this wasn't a problem in ancient Greece. Most writing was designed to be spoken (or even sung!) in front of large crowds, so the written word was often 'heard' far more than it was 'read'.

Though not everyone could read it at the time, the short and organised Greek alphabet ended up being the ancestor of almost every modern European alphabet that came after it – like English. And, if you're reading this book, now you know just how important it was!

The name 'alphabet' comes from the first two letters: alpha and beta. These are our letters A and B.

LET THE GAMES BEGIN

Ever watched the Olympic Games? It's one of the most important sporting events on the planet, bringing together the best sportsmen and women from around the world to compete in amazing physical challenges for all to see.

Athletes wore loincloths in the first Olympic Games. These eventually fell out of fashion and they all competed naked instead!

The Olympics are celebrated every four years, and they begin when an athlete uses a flaming torch to set alight a great cauldron at the Olympic stadium in whichever country is hosting the Games.

Every time the Games are held, a torch is first lit in **Olympia** (the city where it's believed the first Olympic Games were held in 776 BCE) and then carried all the way to the host city. This is a tradition inspired by the ancient Greeks, who carried burning torches to the gods' altars. Back then, the Olympics were a religious festival held in honour of Zeus.

The Olympic Games were huge in ancient Greece, and included events like racing, wrestling, discus, javelin, the long jump and chariot racing. They also involved artistic and theatrical displays. Many athletes trained at the gymnasium, a special centre where young men not only practised sport, but also took lessons in art and science. But don't be fooled by these bookish athletes – one of the most popular events was the **pankration**, which was like a mixed martial art where the only rules were that you weren't allowed to bite your opponent or gouge out their eyes!

Only men were allowed to enter the Olympics ...

... but unmarried girls could take part in the Heraean Games.

These games were organised by a committee of 16 married women and were part of a festival celebrating Zeus's wife, the goddess Hera. Young girls competed in running races, wearing short tunics that exposed one shoulder and one breast.

Despite the importance of the Olympics in ancient Greece, various events – including natural disasters, invasions, the introduction of Christianity and the Romans outlawing 'pagan' festivals in 393 CE – meant that the games gradually disappeared, along with the main temples and monuments of Olympia. They remained a thing of the past until **Pierre de Coubertin**, a French historian, brought them back in 1896.

The winners of the Olympic and Heraean Games each received a wreath made from olive branches, and they were welcomed home as true heroes.

If you've ever been to the theatre, you'll know that the audience usually watches the show in complete silence.

In ancient Greece, it couldn't have been more different! The spectators shouted, heckled the actors, chucked fruit or even started fights!

Despite the rowdy crowds, the Greeks took theatre very seriously. Just like many of their other traditions, the art of theatre had its roots in religious ceremonies, and was an important part of the festivals and rituals held in honour of Zeus's son, Dionysus, the god of wine and fertility. Out of these religious rituals came the plays that we are still able to enjoy today, by playwrights such as **Aeschylus**, **Sophocles** and **Euripides**.

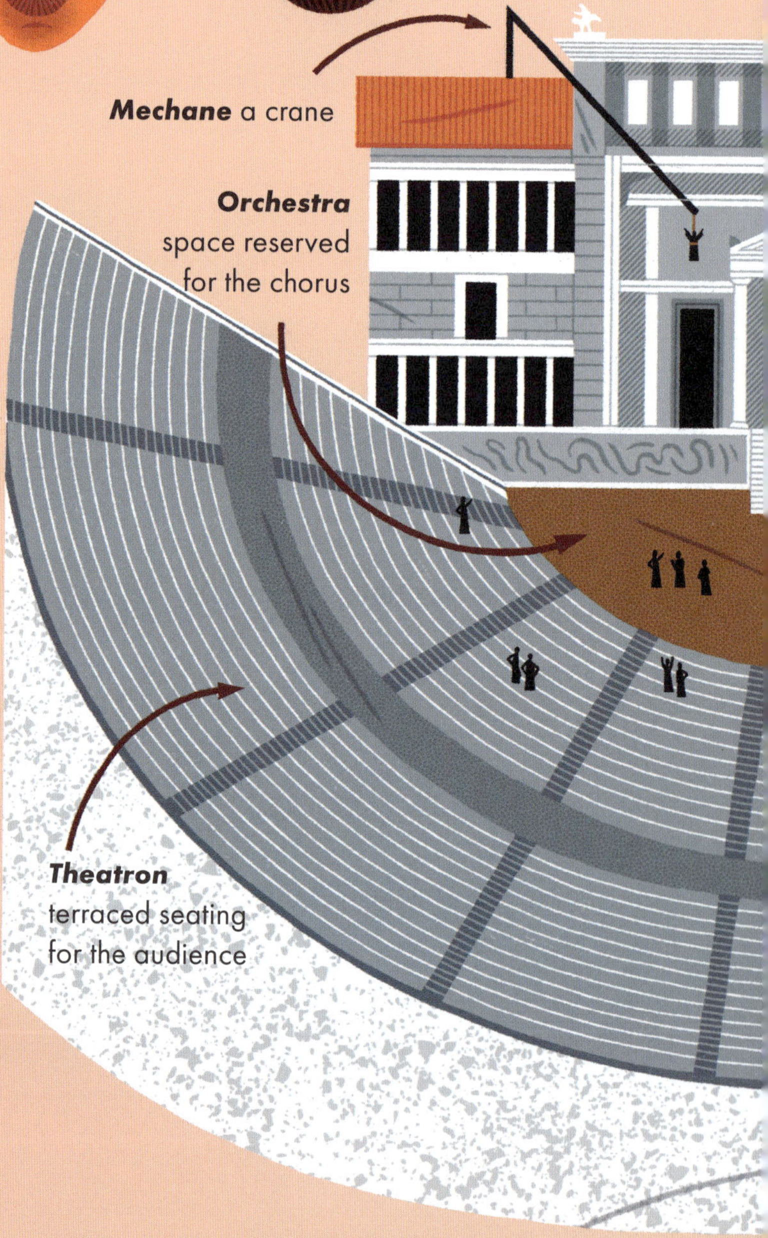

Mechane a crane

Orchestra space reserved for the chorus

Theatron terraced seating for the audience

A STAGE

Let's start the show!

Skene
dressing room

Plays were performed in huge open-air theatres. Some, such as the **Ancient Theatre of Epidaurus**, could hold as many as 15,000 spectators. The acoustics there are so good that when plays are staged in these ancient venues today, people are still surprised how well actors' voices carry in spaces that are so large and open. Not only that, but these places had sophisticated special effects, including cranes to help the actors fly through the air, and trapdoors and tunnels to make them vanish from view.

Some plays featured lots of characters, who would all be played by just a few actors using different masks for the different roles. Alongside the actors was a chorus that would sing and dance in the **orchestra**. Many ancient Greek plays had female main characters, but as women were not permitted to act, these roles were always played by men.

THALES

HERACLITUS

THEANO

SOCRATES

Socrates challenged people to question everything – to be critical thinkers.

ARISTOTLE

PLATO

FROM MYTHOS TO LOGOS

Think that philosophy is boring and has nothing to do with the real world? Well, think again!

One of the most important buildings in ancient Greece was the **Temple of Apollo**, at the sacred site of **Delphi**. According to legend, it was inscribed with the words γνωθι σεαυτόν. Oops, sorry! I forgot it was written in Classical Greek! That means 'know yourself'. This is what philosophy is all about: learning to better understand ourselves and our world.

The first school of Greek philosophy was founded in the city of **Miletus** in the 6th century BCE. Located in what is now Turkey, Miletus was a place where trade was booming. Because of this, it became an ideal base not only for trading goods, but also for people from all around the world to meet and exchange ideas.

These first philosophers – with unique names like **Thales**, **Anaximander** and **Anaximenes** – were interested in the nature (**physis**) of the universe. While most ancient Greeks had relied on myths (**mythos**) to explain why the world was the way it was, these men were the first to try to understand it through debate and reasoning (**logos**).

Then, in the later half of the 5th century BCE, the **sophists** appeared. They were teachers who travelled around Greece's major cities and educated young men. Sophists taught lots of different subjects, like politics and the arts, but they were especially interested in the power of words and the art of persuading others of your point of view.

> **Philosophy invites us to ask questions, seek answers, express our thoughts, expand our horizons and learn to appreciate opinions that are different from our own.**

The famous philosopher **Socrates** was born in Athens in the 5th century BCE. Central to his thinking was the concept of virtue (or **aretē**) and how it could be achieved through knowledge. In order to behave properly, you had to be knowledgeable. Bad behaviour was not seen as a consequence of wickedness, but of ignorance. Socrates was widely admired, but also hated. Accused of corrupting the youth by encouraging them to ask questions, he was sentenced to death in 399 BCE. Sadly, in the past and even today, people have been punished for being independent thinkers.

Although Socrates never wrote a single book, he is still considered one of history's most important philosophers thanks to other philosophers such as **Plato** and **Aristotle** who continued his work.

A SENSE OF HUMOURS

For a long time, ancient Greeks believed that diseases were punishments from angry gods. As such, Greek medicine was steeped in mysticism, and people would turn to priests and their magical rituals for cures. However, from the 6th century BCE, doctors – just like philosophers of the age – began to turn away from supernatural explanations and look to reasoning, observation and experimentation to discover why a person was sick. By breaking with superstition and by building on previous successes from Egypt and Mesopotamia, the Greeks developed a model for understanding human health which would define Western medicine for over a thousand years. It was called **Humourism**.

Popularised by **Hippocrates of Kos**, the most famous of all the Greek doctors, the theory went that the human body contained four important fluids or **humours**.

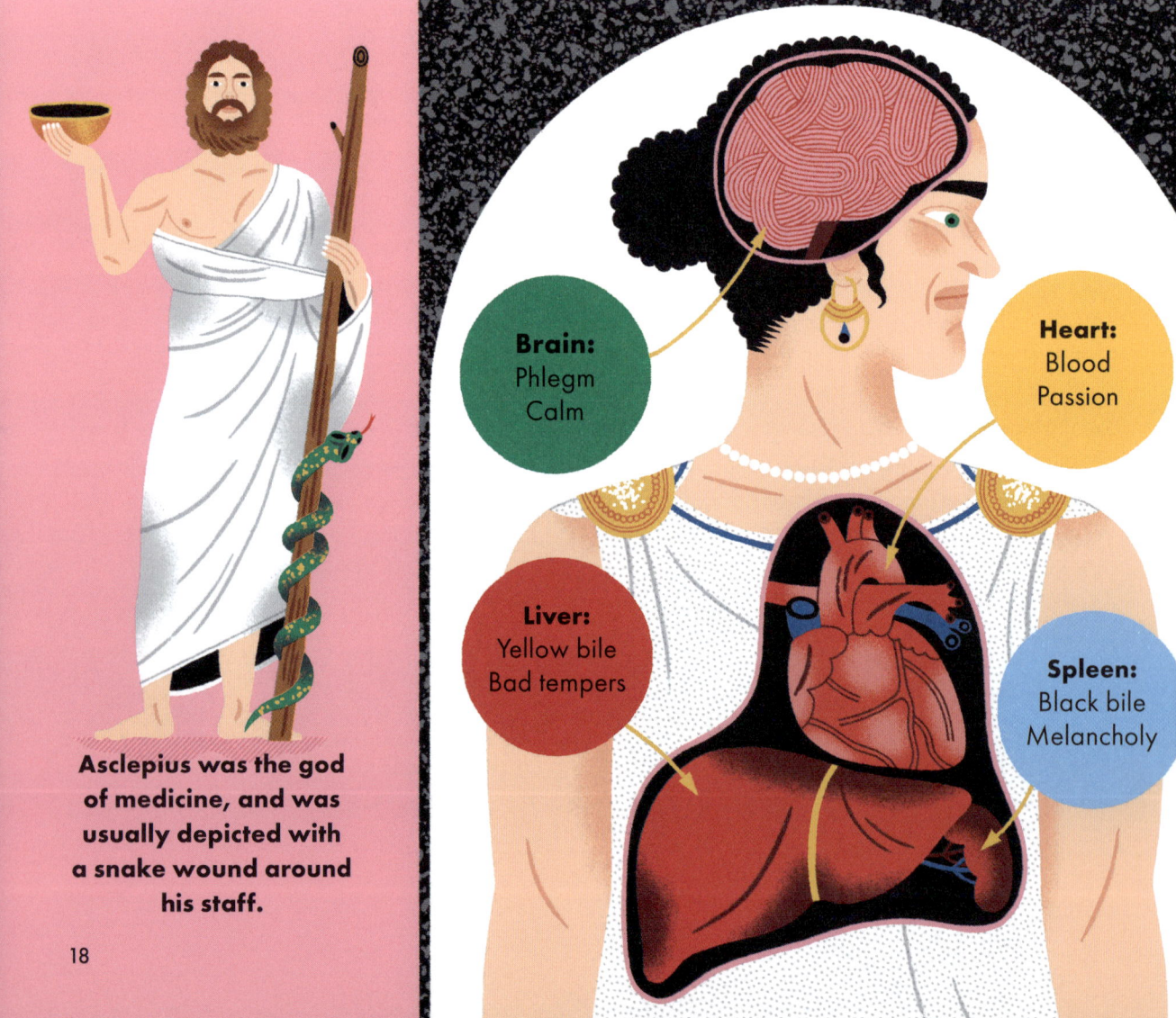

Asclepius was the god of medicine, and was usually depicted with a snake wound around his staff.

Brain:
Phlegm
Calm

Heart:
Blood
Passion

Liver:
Yellow bile
Bad tempers

Spleen:
Black bile
Melancholy

These were blood, phlegm, yellow bile and black bile, which were made in the heart, brain, liver and spleen. Ancient medics believed that someone was in good health when the different parts of the body and their humours were balanced and in harmony.

If these humours were out of balance, a person would get sick or develop different character traits. For example, if someone had a gloomy nature, it was believed they may have had too much black bile, while too much yellow bile would cause bad tempers.

People who were quiet or indifferent had too much phlegm, while those who were passionate and lively had too much blood.

Though we now know that harmful germs, and not imbalanced humours, are the cause of most diseases, Hippocrates championed other ideas we still use today, like how when it comes to sickness, prevention is better than cure. This is why we should live a healthy lifestyle with regular exercise and a balanced diet, and enjoy plenty of rest, fresh air and relaxation.

Hippocrates went to the extreme of personally tasting various bodily fluids like vomit and urine (yuck!).

Asclepius's daughter was Hygieia, the goddess of curing and cleanliness. It's from her that we get the word 'hygiene'.

EUREKA!

Imagine a city under siege from dozens of boats. In the 3rd century BCE, this is what happened to the Greek colony of **Syracuse**, when one of the most powerful armies in the Mediterranean, the Romans, tried to storm the city. Just as all seemed lost, a man called **Archimedes** came to the rescue. From behind the city walls came catapults, and enormous clawed cranes that overturned invading ships. Then, his huge mirrors appeared on the battlements, reflecting sunlight and burning the ships' sails. The Romans were forced to abandon ship, suffering a humiliating defeat. Though the Romans eventually went on to conquer Syracuse, they were fended off for three years thanks to Archimedes' war machines.

Having been written long after the siege occurred, it's possible that parts of Archimedes' story are too good to be true (his surviving writings never included plans for giant claws and heat rays). That said, Archimedes attracted such tall tales because his genius inventions made him a living legend among the Greeks. He was, without a doubt, one of the most important scientists of the ancient world.

The catapult

Defence of Syracuse

Archimedes invented a mechanism to pump water upwards. This is known as the 'Archimedes screw' and it is still used today.

The work of Archimedes highlights just how important science – a rational and methodical way of explaining the world – was to the Greeks. His breakthroughs in areas such as physics, astronomy, medicine and mathematics, together with influences from Eastern civilisations, laid the foundations for modern science.

Archimedes made great contributions to science by carrying out imaginative experiments with spheres, spirals, parabolas, levers, the number pi and **Archimedes' Principle** – a scientific law which helps explain why objects sink or float. Legend has it that Archimedes discovered this law while he was in the bath – he was so happy that he ran around the city naked shouting '**Eureka!**', an expression we still use today to celebrate a new discovery ... though perhaps in a more discreet and modest way than this genius inventor.

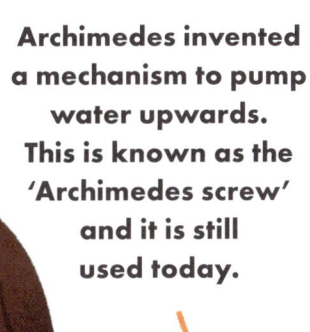

Archimedes' screw

To quote Archimedes, "Give me a place to stand and a lever long enough and I will move the world."

The lever

VISIBLE AND INVINCIBLE

Plato believed that love (or **eros**) was a force that inspired humans to see, do and create beautiful things.

For him, falling in love was about seeking goodness and beauty, something that went far beyond the subject of bodies and gender.

In ancient times, some romantic relationships between men were accepted by society, particularly in aristocratic or military circles.

This was less the case for romantic relationships between women. Such relationships went against much of what Greek society expected of women, which was to marry and have their husband's children.

This is one reason why some women chose to join **thiasoi**, communities where unmarried women lived, recited poetry, learned skills and celebrated religious festivals. It is within these spaces that women likely explored

relationships away from men. **Sappho** was the founder of one such place.

Sappho was a poet, born at the end of the 7th century BCE on the island of **Lesbos**. In her works, she celebrated love and friendship between women, and wrote intense poems about her desires for both men and women.

Sappho wasn't fussed about who we love, or the labels or names we give to our feelings. For her, love was love.

Today, only small pieces of Sappho's works have survived. Legend has it that **Pope Gregory VII** ordered her poems to be burned for being 'immoral' in 1073, but the copies that existed may have simply been damaged or lost over time. However, she was very well-known while she was alive. Statues were made in her honour, and she was celebrated by figures such as Plato, who called her a **muse** (a goddess of the arts).

The word 'lesbian' pays homage to Sappho and her works, as she came from Lesbos.

"What is beautiful is good, and who is good will soon also be beautiful."

"Then love shook my heart like the wind that falls on oaks in the mountains."

Solon

We live in a **representative democracy**. This means people vote in elections to choose which politicians go into power and make the big decisions for the running of the community. This would have horrified the citizens of Athens, whose city is often described as the 'birthplace of democracy'.

The word 'democracy' comes from the Greek *demos* (people) and *kratos* (strength or power).

The people of Athens didn't let any old group of politicians take charge of their country – they ran it themselves! Athenian democracy was a **direct democracy**, meaning that the citizens participated directly in decision-making. Positions of power were pulled out of a hat and rotated, allowing all citizens to take turns in running the city. It was frowned upon not to join in.

THE PEOPLE

There were no slips of paper or electronic forms to cast a vote. Athenians voted by throwing either white or black stones into a bowl.

Pericles

Practising democracy didn't just mean ticking a box on a voting card every few years. It was something the Athenians did every day! They debated constantly – in the street, or in institutes – about the issues that concerned them. Assembly meetings would have as many as 6,000 citizens who would actually fight to get in (everyone had to pay to attend these meetings, so they didn't want to waste their vote *or* their money!).

However, Athenian democracy was still not fair or equal. In order to vote, you had to be a **citizen**.

And that was the problem: who was and who was not a citizen? In Athens, only native-born, free men had citizenship. Slaves, immigrants and women were all denied the right to vote.

THE QUEST OF HEINRICH SCHLIEMANN

In 1876, Schliemann's team believed they had discovered the tomb of King Agamemnon in Mycenae.

Imagine you've just finished watching *The Lord of the Rings* and you decide to go off in search of Middle Earth. Or that after reading *Harry Potter*, you decide you are destined to prove that Hogwarts School of Witchcraft and Wizardry actually exists. Well, in the 19th century, something like that happened to German millionaire **Heinrich Schliemann**.

When he was seven, Schliemann became fascinated by the legendary city of **Troy**, once known as 'Ilion'. According to Homer's poem ***The Iliad***, it had been burned down after a long war between the Trojans and Greeks. Most historians of the time believed that Troy was purely fictional, and only existed in Homer's imagination. Schliemann, however, believed it had been real.

So in 1868, with a copy of *The Iliad* tucked under his arm, Schliemann set out to excavate various sites in Greece and Turkey in the hope of discovering the mythical city of Troy, and to prove that the poem's characters (such as the warrior **Achilles**, the Greek king **Agamemnon** and the beautiful **Queen Helen**) were real people.

After three years (and after spending a lot of money), Schliemann discovered thousands of gold and silver objects at a site on the hill of **Hisarlik**, in what is now Turkey. He named it **Priam's Treasure**, after the mythical **king of Troy**. Schliemann then continued excavating the site and discovered not only the remains of one city, but of different cities dating from between 1500 and 1000 BCE.

Were they actually the ruins of Troy?

Archaeologists today still cannot agree. It is clear that some of the events told by Homer were fictitious, but others do match discoveries made in the region.

Whatever may or may not have happened, what is certain is that Troy still forms a part of our world culture today thanks to Homer. His incredible tale of the Trojan War has inspired and awed countless generations for thousands of years, including one very determined seven-year-old boy!

Alexander the Great is said to have known *The Iliad* off by heart, and to have always carried a copy of it with him. He identified with Achilles, who he hailed as the strongest hero of them all.

On his expeditions, Alexander was accompanied by botanists and geographers, who made lots of fascinating discoveries on the way.

A METEORITE IN THE SKY OF HISTORY

The life of **Alexander the Great** (356–323 BCE) was brief but dazzling, like a meteorite. The son of **Phillip II of Macedonia** and **Olympias of Epirus**, Alexander was taught by the philosopher Aristotle as well as the best teachers of the time. Following his father's death, Alexander took the throne at just 20 years old, but faced several rebellions and had to defeat his rivals to become king. He established his power in Macedonia and throughout the rest of Greece, and then embarked on an extraordinary journey for which he would go down in history – his dramatic expedition towards **Asia**.

Just two years after coming to the throne, Alexander conquered the Anatolian peninsula and the eastern Mediterranean, including Egypt where he was proclaimed pharaoh. Not satisfied with this, he continued his expedition to Persia, defeating **Darius III** and conquering **Persepolis**, the capital of the **Persian empire**. But not even that was enough for Alexander, and in 327 BCE he reached **India**, going further than any Greek had gone before.

Some have claimed that Alexander planned to unite Asia and Europe into one single kingdom. What he didn't know – nor anyone else at the time – was just how big the continent of Asia was. Perhaps if he had known, he wouldn't have taken off on the adventure that took him thousands of miles into unknown lands. Or, considering his ego, perhaps he would. Alexander was driven by a dream of glory from which he never awoke, not even when his most loyal soldiers (who had followed him for over a decade) turned on him and demanded they return home. With his generals returning to Greece, Alexander settled in the city of **Babylon** in 323 BCE, where he died at the age of 32.

Alexander's legacy was one of the largest empires in the ancient world, and also one of the shortest-lived. However, the impact of his journeys, the cities he founded and the cultural exchange he encouraged could never be erased.

TIMELINE

The timeline below – as with all timelines about ancient history – is based on a series of best guesses when it comes to dates, but it serves to order and make sense of when certain events took place.

The origins of ancient Greece can be found in the Minoan culture (on the island of Crete) and the Mycenaean culture (central and southern Greek peninsula). They are considered the direct ancestors of modern Greeks.

From then on, the history of ancient Greece is usually divided into several periods based on historical events and the evolution of artistic forms.

The **Greek Dark Ages** (1200–776 BCE) began with the disappearance of the Mycenaean world. We have very little information about this period (hence the name), but it is characterised by migration, war and epidemics which ravaged the land.

The **Archaic Period** (776–510 BCE) was when the first poleis (city-states) and colonies were formed.

The **Classical Period** (510–323 BCE) is the period of greatest splendour, but also of turbulent wars against the Persians, and between Athenians and Spartans.

The **Hellenistic Period** (323–146 BCE) is from the death of Alexander the Great until the Roman conquest of Greece.

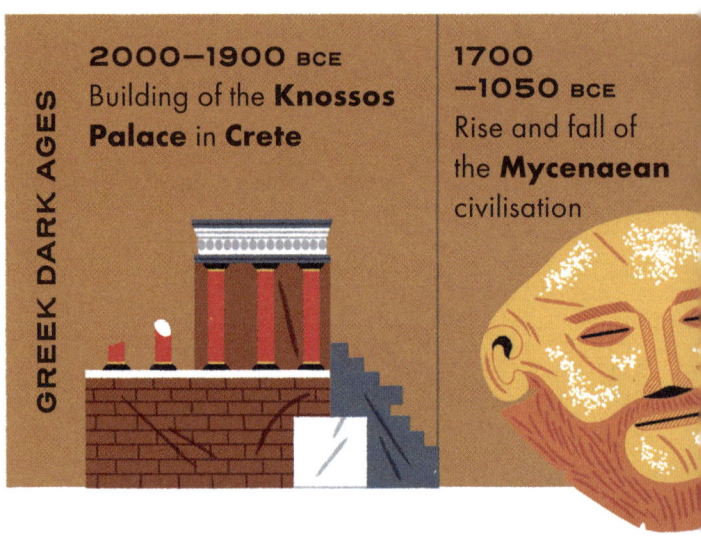

GREEK DARK AGES

2000–1900 BCE
Building of the **Knossos Palace** in **Crete**

1700 –1050 BCE
Rise and fall of the **Mycenaean** civilisation

447 –438 BCE
Building of the **Parthenon**

461 BCE
Pericles comes to power

431–404 BCE
Peloponnesian War

399 BCE
Socrates dies

1350–1300 BCE
Trojan War

ARCHAIC PERIOD

776 BCE
First **Olympic Games**

734 BCE
Founding of **Syracuse**

499–449 BCE
Greco-Persian Wars

CLASSICAL PERIOD

514 BCE
Assassination of **Hipparchus**, the tyrant of Athens

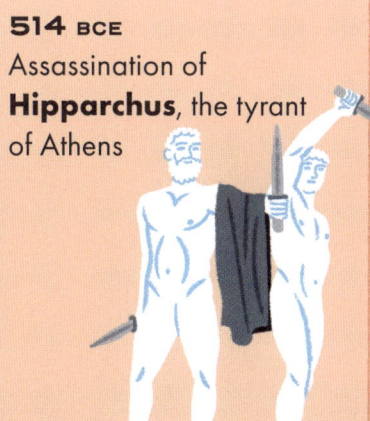

680 BCE
First **coins** are produced

387 BCE
Plato founds the **Academy of Athens**

HELLENISTIC PERIOD

323 BCE
Alexander the Great dies

146 BCE
Battle of **Corinth**, and the defeat of the Greek empire

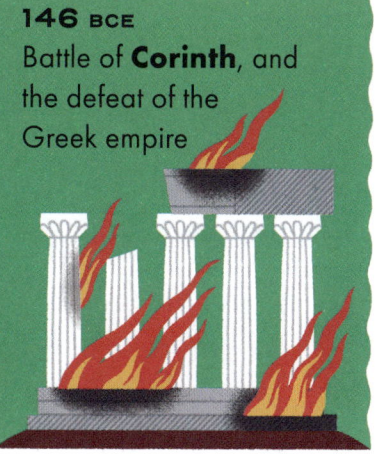

To Pau, my little Heracles – F.L.

BLOOMSBURY CHILDREN'S BOOKS
Bloomsbury Publishing Plc
50 Bedford Square, London WC1B 3DP, UK
Bloomsbury Publishing Ireland Limited
29 Earlsfort Terrace, Dublin 2, D02 AY28, Ireland

BLOOMSBURY, BLOOMSBURY CHILDREN'S BOOKS and the Diana logo are trademarks of Bloomsbury Publishing Plc

First published in Spain 2024 by Alba Editorial S.L.
This edition published in Great Britain 2025 by Bloomsbury Publishing Plc

A catalogue record for this book is available from the British Library

ISBN: HB: 978-1-5266-8630-5; eBook: 978-1-5266-8629-9

10 9 8 7 6 5 4 3 2 1

Printed and bound in China by Toppan Leefung Printing

To find out more about our authors and books visit www.bloomsbury.com and sign up for our newsletters
For product safety related questions contact productsafety@bloomsbury.com